THE HEART OF TEACHING

Encouragement For Showing Love And Respect To Your Students

DANA KWIATKOWSKI

LAEL PUBLISHING

THE HEART OF TEACHING
Encouragement For Showing Love And Respect To Your Students
by Dana Kwiatkowski
Published by The Lael Agency
Winston Salem, North Carolina
www.LaelAgency.com

No part of this book may be used or reproduced in any form, stored in a retrieval system, or transmitted in any form by any means, electronic, photocopy, mechanical, recording or otherwise without written permission from the author. The only exception is for critical articles or reviews, in which brief excerpts may be used.

Paperback ISBN - 978-1-7337569-0-7

Author's contact information
Email: Dana@TheHeartofTeaching.us
Website: TheHeartofTeaching.us

Copyright © 2021 by Dana Kwiatkowski

All Rights Reserved

First Edition

Printed in the United States of America.

Dedicated to the greatest blessings in my life - Dave, Paul, John, Amy, Katlyn and Virginia and the many pets who have enriched our lives,

and to my wonderful colleagues who consistently show love and respect to their students.

With thanks to David Roop, for your honest and creative evaluation of my manuscript.

CONTENTS

Chapter 1, Page 9
How I Entered the World of Education

Chapter 2, Page 17
What Shaped My View Of Teaching?

Chapter 3, Page 23
How Do We View Our Students?

Chapter 4, Page 31
Dealing With Behavior And Personal Needs

Chapter 5, Page 35
How Should We View Ourselves And Our Jobs?

Chapter 6, Page 41
Working With Administrators And Other Teachers

Chapter 7, Page 49
How My Teaching Can Make A Difference

Chapter 8, Page 55
Specifically In The Classroom

Chapter 9, Page 67
More Tangible Things I Can Do

Chapter 10, Page 75
The Parent-Teacher Partnership

Chapter 11, Page 81
Daily Reminders To Help Us Keep The Proper Perspective

Chapter 12, Page 85
Conclusion

Chapter 1

HOW I ENTERED THE WORLD OF EDUCATION

I didn't grow up dreaming of becoming a teacher. In fact, I don't remember ever thinking about working with young people at all until I was newly out of college and began helping at my church by putting together musicals and programs for the children. While I had initially gotten into this endeavor because of my love of music, I quickly realized that I really had fun working with kids. As soon as one musical ended, I would actively begin searching for another one to start practicing because seeing these kids excel was so rewarding for me.

Despite my love of this work, though, I didn't even consider the possibility of working with children at first. In fact, up through high school I had gained the approval of adults by saying that I wanted to be a doctor. At that point in my life, the approval of other people was the most important thing to my mind, and for me to think of being anything different than this initial plan would have been to settle for less – though of course, I've since seen that this isn't true at all. How I could have used a kind word of truth spoken by a caring teacher during high school to help me realize that every path is of equal value, that it doesn't matter at all what other people think is impressive, and that I should at least explore the many possibilities available to me!

    Still, I was a top student in high school and won a scholarship to attend Wake Forest University – where I quickly found that everyone else there was a top high school student also. In fact, a solid 40% of the freshman class were going into pre-med and planned to be doctors, just like I was. What a wake-up call this was for me! I had been able to perform well in high school without much studying, but things were very different in college! In every class, the standards were extremely high and I had to learn quickly how to take notes well, read efficiently, and study effectively. As hard as college was, though, I still held on to the notion that medical school was what I wanted and anything else – either in the medical field or out of it, for that matter – was just not good enough. I do remember thinking, maybe wistfully, that teaching was something I thought I would really enjoy. I also remember being envious of my peers who were science and education majors, both because they seemed to enjoy classes that offered practical life applications (so much more than mine in Cell Biology, Microbiology, Organic Chemistry, and Physiology seemed to do at the time) AND because they knew they would always have summers off while non-teachers worked year-round.

    After I graduated with my degree in Biology, I spent

a summer with missionaries who worked among the Zulu people in Izingolweni, Natal, in the Republic of South Africa. This experience had a profound effect on me as I realized – maybe for the first time ever, and definitely for the first time before my own eyes – the extreme injustices perpetrated through racism and colonialism. I don't think I would ever look at people in the same way after seeing how little the Zulu people had and how few opportunities they had to improve their lives. Regardless of how poor these people were, though, they were always so welcoming and friendly, and I gained such an appreciation and high level of respect for them. Then at the end of a wonderful summer I reluctantly returned home to North Carolina and got a job working as a laboratory technician in an oncology lab at a medical research center. At the time, my plan was to begin applying to medical schools and prepare to start an advanced degree the following fall.

In my free time, though, I began the role mentioned above, working with teenagers in a musical ensemble at my church. Before long, I realized that I absolutely loved being with these kids! I loved everything about preparing a production, but the best takeaway for me was seeing each individual teenager's progress and the greatly increased confidence they had at the end of each production.

On the job front, while working in a research hospital with rats and cancer patients, I quickly found that instead of investing myself in the research I was working on, I was constantly thinking about the students I worked with in my volunteer position, like how I could encourage them and how I could help them learn the musicals faster. Between this and many frustrating interactions with the cancer patients whom I couldn't help, I came to realize that the medical field was not for me. So, after a year in the lab, I quit with great relief and returned to Wake Forest to obtain a teaching license in science: specifically, in biology.

    After obtaining my license, my career path in education took many branches. My first position was as a long-term substitute for biology and English in a public high school, where I was first exposed to international students. Kirsten, an exchange student from Norway in one of my classes, was delightful and helped me begin seeing the difficulties of learning in a second language. I still treasure a Norwegian Christmas doll that her mother sent me that year! I also had a Vietnamese student who had escaped the post-war chaos by herself and somehow made it to the United States. Tuyet was precious, hard-headed, and badly scarred emotionally from her experiences. I was able to spend a lot of time with Tuyet as I helped her with both schoolwork and English language acquisition, and I also got to know her ESL (English as a Second Language) teacher well, since I was constantly asking for advice on how best to support Tuyet.
    After this substitute teaching position ended, because of my commitment to help Tuyet, the ESL director asked me to take a position as an ESL tutor for Cambodian, Laotian, and Vietnamese refugee teenagers in another high school. In this position, students came to me several times a day for help with their subjects, and they were always so appreciative of any help I could offer. They had to work so much harder than their American peers, yet they were so grateful for the opportunities that they had

been given here in America. This experience opened my eyes to the needs of refugees as well as their tenacity and hopes; it also led me to develop a deep, lifelong respect for all immigrants, whether they are coming to the United States or other countries. Since then, I have often had the thought that my own family could have been in that same position of needing to flee our home, if we had lived in a politically unstable country. Moreover, how could anyone want anything other than the best life for their children?

When that semester of tutoring ended, I went back to graduate school at the University of North Carolina at Chapel Hill and earned a Master of Science degree in Public Health, specifically in Medical Parasitology and Laboratory Practice. Why this degree and not a Master of Arts in Teaching? It was extremely important to me that I get a master's degree in my subject area of biology, and after having both worked with refugees and spent time in an impoverished area in Africa, I was very interested in learning more about the situations in third world countries. I did think that I would like to work in a hospital in a third world country or with the Centers for Disease Control (CDC), but right around the time I graduated with that second degree, the US public health budget was cut drastically, so jobs in that field became scarce. Though this had been my initial plan, then, the change was fine for me: deep down, I was quite ready to get back into the classroom.

After graduate school, my next teaching position was in a public high school that gave me the opportunity of planning an entire year of a biology curriculum using personal computers in the classroom as much as possible. For younger teachers who can't imagine teaching without computers or the internet, this was in 1983 when computers were still novel, and educators were trying to figure out just how they could be used to enhance learning.

The school that this program was in had many students who received no support from home, so I quickly learned firsthand just how important a teacher's affirming words were.

During the years I taught here, I was also invited to be a faculty member at The Governor's School of North Carolina. This gave me an incredible opportunity each summer to teach Natural Science on the campus of Salem College. I had attended The Governor's School one summer during my high school years and loved my time there, so of course I was happy to be back in that "think tank" atmosphere and interacting with creative thinkers every day. The Governor's School was founded on the premise that students with strong intellectual and creative abilities can succeed far beyond the norm when they are provided with thoughtful challenges and opportunities. This premise of high expectations has greatly shaped my own teaching style, and from then on, I began trying to include critical thinking challenges in my own lessons as often as I could.

I stayed in the Computer Biology position at the public high school for five years, then moved to South Carolina so that my husband could attend graduate school. While in South Carolina, I was hired for a job with a schedule most teachers only dream of: I became one of three Gifted and Talented (GT) Coordinators in the GT program of a 3000-student high school in Richland County. In practical terms, this meant that I taught three seminar classes in the morning and had the rest of the day to research and plan lessons for those classes. I could hardly believe that I was being compensated for time to plan lessons, and I was amazed at how much fun it was to plan for these gifted students when I actually had time to think and collaborate with other professionals. The teachers I worked with there also taught with the same high expectations that I had experienced as a student myself at The Governor's School and were great mentors who helped me interweave unique topics, such as different movie genres or the '60s, with practical applications and challenging assignments.

That job was amazing, but I was more than happy to step away for a bit when our first child was born: I found that I wanted to stay home and raise him during those formative years. Soon after our child was born, my husband completed his graduate courses and we moved back to North Carolina where he took a job as a computer systems analyst. 16 months after our first son was born, we welcomed our second son, and then 21 months after that, our daughter.

When our daughter was 12 months old, I was offered the chance to teach one AP Biology class at our local school system's Career Center. This class, which started at 7:05 am each day, was my first foray into the AP world, and thankfully I had two incredible mentors there who helped guide me along. I was able to do this for two years until the student numbers dropped and the class was no longer needed.

While I taught in this position, my class was made up of Highly Gifted and Talented sophomores who had chosen to add not just an extra class to their day, but also an AP class at that. They were so bright and engaged and just soaked up all the information I had to offer, but they also brought their own needs and hurts to the classroom, which gave me lots of opportunities to show them how much they each had to offer as individuals, not just as students in a class. I remember hosting them at our home for a cookout after the AP exam and hearing how much it meant to them to be invited to a teacher's home.

Looking back, I just hope I adequately expressed to them how much I enjoyed all those early morning meetings with them!

Chapter 2

WHAT SHAPED MY VIEW OF TEACHING?

While the degrees and the early teaching experience were both important, I would actually consider having my own children as the most formative part of my teacher education. As I experienced the love and fierce protective drive of a parent on a daily basis, it hit me one day that I had been looking at my students with an incomplete understanding of their value and worth. All of a sudden, I realized that I shouldn't be viewing students as just young people who were fun to be with, and who would be shaped and directed by my efforts. Instead, I realized, they were also someone else's precious children who were just as deserving of my love and effort as my own children.

As I began wrapping my head around this life-changing thought, I also remember thinking that no one should teach until they have children of their own. Now, I know that thought is totally impractical in reality, but for me, this was one of those moments when I realized how many things about my own teaching would change. Don't get me wrong...I still think that I was a good teacher before I had my own children and came to this realization! In fact, the yearbook at the school where I taught that first Computer Biology program was dedicated to me one year, and I was also inducted into Phi Delta Kappa, the national education honor society. However, the responsibility I felt for my students deepened greatly after I had my own children.

When they reached the age to begin school, my husband and I decided to teach our children at home. When making this decision, we weren't driven by negative thoughts about the schools available; it was more that we had seen the benefits of not being bound to a school day or year schedule, and we wanted to experience these benefits ourselves. We were able to complete schoolwork by lunchtime so the children could play outside and have more time to "just be kids." We were also free to travel during the traditional school months and experience places during the less busy tourist times. Homeschooling was definitely a team effort - my husband actually taught our first child how to read during the mornings while I was teaching AP Biology. Homeschooling was also just a natural lifestyle to move into as I was already staying home with our children at the time and my nature was to view just about everything as a teachable moment. (My apologies to Paul, John, and Amy for this!) I LOVED teaching my own children and being involved with other homeschooling families. Working with other parents who were as committed to education as we were meant that this was a wonderful experience. I was able to use my training as a teacher to lead and teach in homeschool co-ops, and I was often able to help other parents with problems they had encountered while teaching their children. Working one-on-one with my own children also helped me develop strategies for accommodating different ways of learning that I still use in the classroom today.

We homeschooled our oldest son through 11th grade and our two younger children through 8th grade. Then the summer after we finished up homeschooling, I received a phone call from a principal at a local Charlotte Mason private school. He was looking for a part-time music teacher, and after several conversations, I was invited to take the position. It was the perfect fit in so many ways – music has always been a passion of mine and I had spent many years on the music staff of different churches as well as teaching music in homeschooling co-ops and piano through individual lessons. So this was a natural extension of my teaching career.

What an incredible experience it was to work at that school! It was a very small institution, relatively speaking, since it only had 200 students enrolled in grades K - 8, so it felt close-knit and welcoming. It was exciting to step into this role in a school that had the family spirit of a homeschool co-op! It was also a fit for the way I preferred to teach, too: the commitment to give students the absolute best education in spiritual, emotional, and academic terms was extremely strong, and the administration did everything they could to encourage and equip their teachers to give the students their very best. Though I had been teaching for years by that point, I had never experienced an atmosphere quite like this one. The faculty members were driven by a strong and sincere belief that every child is uniquely designed and worthy of every effort we could make to educate them, helping each one develop into a well-rounded adult. Every part of the school program was designed purposely to foster students' success in every area. Parents were also very involved in the school and worked closely with teachers to make the school year a positive experience.

I also learned much from the staff here about turning students' questionable choices into life lessons about consequences, responsibility, and respect. The evidence of lessons learned by students who attended this school manifested itself at my next teaching position as well, since there I had the privilege of teaching a number of high school students who had attended the Charlotte Mason school through middle school. For the most part, they were some of the most respectful and involved students I have ever taught at the high school level.

At the end of my second year in this position, I was approached by the administration of another local private high school about joining their faculty to teach science in a full-time position. It was very difficult to leave my music position, but I was also interested in working full-time and of course, the fact that I would get to teach science all day was a definite draw, so I made the switch back to high school. It was wonderful to be back at the high school level, both because of the curriculum and because of working with the older teens.

Peace Haven Day School (not the real name, for privacy purposes) was a Pre-K 2 through 12th grade school completed with a college preparatory high school, and it had high standards and advanced curricula. This means extra work for a teacher, of course, but also the exhilaration of knowing you are teaching at an advanced level with all the additional challenges that brings. As is the case with any private high school, teachers at Peace Haven wore many hats, so before long, I was working with the student worship team for their weekly chapel time, sponsoring several clubs, planning the freshman trip, and taking on just about any other requests that came my way. After 10 years at Peace Haven I was a senior class sponsor, had planned the senior trip to Costa Rica twice, had taught three different AP classes, and was chair of the Science Department, along with holding numerous other duties. I love teaching at this school, where I have had the wonderful privilege of teaching alongside some of the best teachers I have ever encountered.

All along this circuitous route into and out of, then back into teaching, I was constantly learning more about what good teaching involved – and, in particular, how to manage a classroom so that learning could happen. In each situation I encountered, there were role models for every kind of teacher.

Early in my career, I came across far too many teachers who managed their classrooms through sarcasm and putdowns, and others who showed movies far too often rather than do the work needed to actively teach their students. To be fair, the school where I worked for 5 years after graduate school had far more than its share of discipline problems, but that is still no excuse for teachers to discourage their students. And the difference was important: there were teachers known for how hard their classes were academically, and there were teachers who were characterized as unfair and uncaring. Likewise, there were teachers who had no discipline and no structure to their class times, either because they hadn't yet learned the value of good classroom management or because they didn't really want to be in the classroom and so just didn't care.

I truly think some of these teachers were misguided into thinking students liked having lots of free time and no work in classes, but my experience has taught me that students both like and need structure. Most also enjoy the fact that they are learning something and moving ahead every day. On the positive side, there were also far more teachers who modeled incredibly successful skills and were loved and respected by their students even though the students had to work hard in the class. I loved watching these teachers and trying to figure out what they did that worked so well. What made their classes so interesting that students couldn't wait to take those subjects with them? And why did students feel so accepted in those particular classrooms that they felt confident enough to ask questions?

This book is a compilation of traits and best practices that I have observed in outstanding teachers throughout the last 35 years and incorporated into my own teaching in my lifelong journey toward becoming the best teacher I can be. These traits and practices have blended together in my thinking to shape the way I regard students, and thus, the way I treat them both within and beyond my

What Shaped My View Of Teaching?

classroom. Because of this evolution of my perspective, I have grown to sincerely love and respect my students, and this has made all the difference in my success as a teacher! It is my hope that this book will help other teachers come to see the value and worth of each student so that we can all truly improve the lives and outlooks of our students, supporting them during their development into happy, adjusted, productive adults.

THE HEART OF TEACHING

Chapter 3

HOW DO WE VIEW OUR STUDENTS?

A teacher's feelings toward their students will, of course, deeply shape the way that the teacher will treat them. I'm sure that we've all experienced classrooms where the teacher's pets were painfully obvious. I remember wondering throughout elementary school if I would ever know what it felt like to be one of these favored students - and then in the 6th grade I had the wonderful Miss Brown. Everyone in her class felt special and respected, rather than some lucky few being singled out. To this day I can remember many specific details of that class because I knew she valued me, thought I was smart, and gave me many chances to develop my abilities. Miss Brown was a true gift from God for me, as my 5th grade teacher had made it clear, in many tangible and intangible ways, that she did not like me. In Miss Brown's room, suddenly I was a good artist and instead of getting a D in handwriting, I earned a B because Miss Brown understood left-handed writers.

    Miss Brown also had a profound respect for her students, and this came across so clearly in the encouragement she gave us and her obvious enjoyment of teaching us. Her view of students was that we were precious creations and someone else's much-loved children. She viewed us as adults-in-training and helped us look ahead to becoming responsible world citizens. She shared world events in a conversational way like she just assumed that we would be interested, so of course we did become interested. This was in the late '60s, and I remember becoming aware of pollution that year as she talked about how smog was formed and how all the cars being driven and the companies releasing waste products were filling the air with dangerous particles and chemicals. I didn't realize then how far ahead of the times she was - I just knew that she was concerned, and she thought we were old enough to understand that concern.

    That year we never minded rainy days when we couldn't go out on the playground because that just meant we could play our favorite game - Cars! Miss Brown would direct the rearrangement of desks to form roads and intersections, and we all became either cars, traffic lights, or policemen. I learned a lot of driving laws simply by playing that game. I'm sure it was a lot of work for Miss Brown to rearrange the classroom for us, but she always acted as excited as we felt, getting to play Cars.

    I also remember how much she involved the class in decisions that affected us. After studying Asia, she proposed that we buy a print of Japanese art to put up in our classroom. She let us vote on the painting to buy, collected our coins, and sent in the order for us. When that painting was hung, we felt quite grown up and accomplished. So many life lessons were learned in that simple activity – diplomacy and compromise, saving money for a common goal, and respecting others' choices.

Viewing students as precious, unique creations who deserve our greatest respect can revolutionize our classrooms. When we start seeing them as adults in the making and realize that we have been given not only a tremendous responsibility but also a tremendous gift to be able to steer them toward good decisions, suddenly every word we speak and every activity we do in our classrooms carries a much greater importance and deserves the best planning. When I put myself in my students' shoes and try to imagine their experiences in my class, suddenly the things like any sarcasm that I might want to express, the subtle or not-so-subtle belittling comments, and the lack of compassion or of attention that I might be tempted to show become huge impediments to their success. By shifting my thinking this way, I also realize just how rude my "cute" comments can seem. The hours of preparation I might have spent, all the brainstorming and planning about how to make the lesson fun, inviting, and interesting – none of that will bring about any results if the students do not feel respected and valued while learning the lesson.

It is also worth noting that a wonderful phenomenon exists within the human brain where when we act with respect toward our students, even if we actually don't feel that way initially, we will help ourselves develop this respect for them. Dr. Richard Wiseman, a British psychology professor, has brought this phenomenon to the forefront with his book *The As If Principle: The Radically New Approach to Changing Your Life*. This psychological principle establishes that our actions can dictate our emotions and feelings, which is a radical switch from the well-established idea that our actions almost always result from our feelings. The latter is obviously true and experienced by almost everyone almost every day, but the "As If " principle shows us yet another means that we have with which to show our students the respect they deserve – even when we don't feel like showing it. The perception that students have of how you as their teacher view them can tremendously impact how they receive and engage with your teaching.

Imparting knowledge or guiding students to where information can be found are just two small parts of the whole of teaching, though. This thought reminds me of what is stated in I Corinthians 13: "If I do anything without love, it is wasted effort." This applies to teaching too because if our goal is to prepare our students to be productive adults, then we must take a long-term view of our task and provide a caring, encouraging atmosphere while also imparting knowledge.

With this thought in mind, I need to weigh in here on a well-known adage often quoted in teacher training classes. I know I'll probably be stepping on toes here, but I totally disagree with the "don't smile until 2nd quarter" mandate for good classroom management. I think this clearly conveys a message of "I can't trust you and I don't respect you" and even "I don't like you" to students. Instead, establishing a few all-encompassing rules such as "Show

Respect to Each Other and to School Property," discussing what that rule actually involves, and demonstrating that respect is are usually all I have needed to start off the year in a positive manner. It has been a rare occurrence for a student to respond negatively to an encouraging atmosphere and even when that has happened, there is always a hurtful history or difficult circumstances the student is bringing to the classroom that have caused this negative response. So, to beginning teachers what I would say instead is: make sure you enforce what few rules you make and ensure that students understand how this enforcement is for the good of the class as a whole.

Still, of course we've all had those students in our classes who behave in a manner that does not maintain a great learning environment. For the inexperienced teacher, this issue can overwhelm every other aspect of the classroom experience, since the behavior of the students drives the class. The new teacher also often views this as total disrespect and in order to deal with it quickly so that class can continue, they might resort to a put-down or to shaming the student into behaving. As every new teacher also learns eventually, this may quash the bad behavior for the moment, but it does nothing for solving the actual problem at the heart of such behavior. This isn't a book about discipline techniques, so I'm not going to get into that aspect of classroom management skills too deeply, but I will say that if you can deal with these situations with humor or a light-hearted response, often the student relaxes and becomes part of the classroom community. Remind yourself often that it is not your job to "put someone in their place." Oftentimes a whispered question of "Is everything okay?" is enough to give the student time to reset and save face. Of course, there will be times, unfortunately, when the disruption is so great that it must be dealt with immediately, with firmness and discipline. Just make sure that later you come back to what happened with the class or the students involved and try to help them learn from what happened. Often just getting the student to look at what they said or did from a different perspective is all it takes to make sure incidents like this don't happen again.

At the same time, don't feel you must deal with difficult students on your own. Ask for help early in the year before you get to feeling like you've lost control completely. Other teachers may have already figured out how to work with that student and you can learn from them. It is never a sign of weakness to ask other teachers or the school administration for help. Just don't let a bad situation go too long before dealing with it. You don't want a negative situation with one or a few students to dictate the classroom experience for the rest of your class.

An important guiding principle for me in these kinds of situations is to never let a confrontation between me and a student escalate to a battle of wills. Don't become so rigid in a situation that you can get backed into a corner when a student refuses to cooperate.   Try to deal with situations with humor or kindness, always giving the student an out. If you don't allow the student to back up and right their wrong without losing face, then you will lose any bit of trust you may have built. Put yourself in their place and try to offer them the grace that you would want offered to you if you were in that mindset. I have sent upset students on errands, or quietly suggested that they walk up and down the hall a few times. I've even given students who can't seem to pull it together some change to go to the vending machine. Kindness and respect for the fact that life is a little hard for them right now will show your students that you care for them beyond their enrollment in your class, and also that you understand they are more than just the difficult day they are having. That being said, I do think it is important too for you to explain at some point how their behavior negatively impacts the class so they can hopefully see the bigger picture. Determine that you will find the good in a student who is not behaving well. Point out something good you see in them and tell them plainly how much that good attribute of theirs contributes to a great class for you and their classmates.

    A former principal gave me some of the best advice I have ever been given regarding dealing with difficult students. I remember sitting in her office one day lamenting that I had tried everything I had in my arsenal to win over a certain student, but that the bottom line was that I just did not like the student and so was struggling to be nice. After hearing this, she said simply, "Well, try praying for him every day." So I did, and before long I could honestly say I loved the kid and was doing all I could to help him be successful. There is an old saying that proves true here: "It's hard to kick someone when you are down on your knees."

    Two years ago, my husband and I had the privilege of providing a home for a teenage boy who was a refugee from South Sudan. When we opened our home to him, our hope was to provide a stable, loving home for him along with academic encouragement and support so he could successfully matriculate at Peace Haven Day School. I had already been tutoring this boy, trying to help him catch up to where he was supposed to be based on his transcripts, and it hadn't taken more than a few sessions with him to realize that his situation was vastly different than the one his transcripts from Africa painted. After psychological testing, we realized that this 18-year-old was at a second grade reading level and had an IQ on the line between borderline and extremely low. We will never know the causes for his low abilities, but this revelation shed light on why he was so far behind, didn't have the foundational knowledge needed to learn in his high school classes, and didn't seem to understand how much he didn't know. What I was unprepared for – and amazed to see – was how my colleagues, his teachers, went all out to help this young man right where he was. They gave him assignments he could do, paired him with students who helped him and listened to him, encouraged him, and took joy in telling me of his successes. Despite his cognitive limitations, his teachers led him to make greater achievements than I had ever thought possible. They were determined to show him respect and help him see his worth. What a great example of making teaching all about the student!

Chapter 4

DEALING WITH BEHAVIOR AND PERSONAL NEEDS

I already mentioned the following thought earlier, but it is so profoundly true that I want to talk about it in greater detail too. One important principle to remember as a teacher is that bad behavior or rude comments don't usually happen without an underlying force driving them. In addition, that behavior usually is not directed at you intentionally or with malice, and it should not be taken as a personal affront. Understanding this was probably the second most important insight I had that shaped my dealings with students. We need to realize that the student who says something rude or disrespectful may have had a horrible morning at home, is upset about something, or doesn't feel well – and in these cases, a calm, relaxed response from you and a kind talk after class may be all this student needs in order to gain a better perspective on things.

I can't even begin to say how much the insights I have gained by talking with students after class have helped me become a kinder, more compassionate person and a better teacher. I know now that if I approach a student in an accusatory manner, then all I will get back is an angry response. But if I show respect and concern when asking a disruptive student how things are going, then I might learn about parents separating or fighting, a loved one losing a job, money troubles, or illness in the family. Any one of these, or other reasons, can explain what might look like out-of-control behavior in the classroom. Oftentimes, children and even young adults have had very few experiences with adults who care for and respect them, so they don't even know how to interact in a non-confrontational, non-defensive way. Knowing that a personal hurt might be underlying problematic behavior can help you put things into perspective and not feel personal offense.

At the same time, some additional important things to keep in mind when you are told these very personal things are 1) make sure you keep that student's confidence unless they have asked for help or are in immediate danger, 2) let them know you are always available to listen, and 3) DON'T promise to help them unless it is something you can actually do or unless you know a resource or an organization that can help. More than anything, students usually just need to talk and have someone listen. Also remember that, unless there is abuse or neglect that you have a legal obligation to report, then it is not your place to get involved in a family's issues. If you feel something is going on that needs to be addressed, then pass that on to a guidance counselor or your principal. It is their job to work on this more closely, and if necessary, to pass that information on to people who are trained to deal with these deeper issues. After you have reported the problem you need to, your job is to teach that student and to provide a safe, comfortable learning environment, not to rescue them. This may sound harsh, but I speak from much experience in wanting to fix every situation for every student. If you get involved more deeply than you can actually fix – emotionally, physically, or financially – then you will be stealing from the emotional energy that needs to go to your own family, yourself, and your job, and you will be getting the student's own hopes up for something that may never happen. In the end, you will be less effective in every area because you are devoting so much thought and effort to something you cannot change anyway. It really does take a village to bring up a child, and this is not your sole responsibility even as a teacher.

    There are many published studies documenting the effect that traumatic events in a child's life may have on their behavior, attitude, and academic progress. I encourage all fellow teachers to take the time to read some of these so that they can better understand the needs of their students. Some excellent material dealing with these issues has come out of the Adverse Childhood Experiences Study conducted by the Centers for Disease Control and Kaiser Permanente (https://www.cdc.gov/violenceprevention/aces/index.html). This study's main findings can be found on numerous other websites as well. These findings are both eye-opening and sobering, and they need to be taken seriously as we seek to help our students reach their fullest potential.

    Often when I see poor behavior becoming a pattern

and I talk with the student to try to figure out what is going on and to help them see what they are doing, I realize that the student is struggling with an issue that is overwhelming them. It may be a class level that is too difficult, a family issue with parents or siblings, sick grandparents, working too late to make ends meet, or struggles with another teacher. When I tell the student sincerely that I am here for them, that I will be praying for them, and that if they will work on their behavior in class that I will do all I can to help them succeed, I have seen overnight changes in their behavior, demeanor, and attitude. Sometimes all a kid needs to know is that someone is looking out for them. Just make sure you follow through with whatever you promise them, and you will see a life changed.

Chapter 5

HOW SHOULD WE VIEW OURSELVES AND OUR JOBS?

As a teacher perhaps even more than any other profession, I can either view my job as an incredible opportunity or I can view it as a chore that I have to get through, day after day. The phrase "an attitude of gratitude" may be overused in our chosen career, but still – this attitude is so appropriate and necessary. The frame of mind with which you enter both lesson preparation and the classroom will definitely be apparent to your students. One thought that always works to turn my thoughts back to gratitude is that, through no merit of my own, I have been given the incredible gift of being born in a free country that offers education and subsequently a choice of life's work to all. I could have been born in an oppressive country ruled by a terrible dictator, with limited schooling opportunities, and without much possibility of pursuing a meaningful career in life, but through no merit of my own I have had the privilege of being a citizen of the United States instead.

Likewise, when I sense that an attitude of entitlement is taking root within the hearts of my students, we go back to the basic thought expressed above and I ask them what they did to deserve being born here. What makes them more deserving than the young person their age in South Sudan who doesn't know where their next meal is coming from, or when the rebels or soldiers will come back to their village on a killing spree? (Also, while we are on this thought, this is a powerful way to address the hatred of refugees and "others" when it surfaces in your class – because almost inevitably, it will.) We are no better and no different than the people who are simply trying to find a better, safer life in the United States for their families. I have told my students that if my children were facing the violence of the drug culture in Latin America or the wars in Yemen, Syria, or South Sudan, then I too would do anything I needed to in order to get them to a safer place. We as teachers have a responsibility to show our students the views of people in other situations in order to help them better understand why certain decisions are made and actions are taken.

Back to the main thought, though: knowing how incredibly I have been blessed, how could I not want to perform all aspects of my job as well as I can and impart all the benefits of education to my students?

Teaching is **all about the students.** This is such a difficult perspective to keep when we have worked so purposefully and diligently to become teachers, to keep up in our fields, and to keep up with educational trends. At times it becomes hard not to view the job in terms of our goals and our plans, or as framed by requirements from administrators, but at its heart, what goes on in the classroom is **all about the students.**

Yes, we are in charge of keeping order to ensure learning, and we put in hours of work to learn the material, then hours more in preparing our presentation of the material to make the big bucks for preparing the next generation and thus determining the fate of our society. (Just kidding about the big bucks, of course!) But in the end, the bottom line is what our students have learned and how it has prepared them to be contributing members of society. If we can play a small role in developing well-educated, confident, and stable young adults, then we should be grateful that our careers bring us a chance to make a difference for the better. We shouldn't need to feel that it is all about us.

Okay, I hope I've made my point that this whole classroom thing is not about us. So, where does that place us in the big picture of education? Well, actually, we are *outside* the big picture. This is because we as teachers are the ones directing everything that goes on in order to make that big picture all about our students.

The way that we think about ourselves greatly impacts our ability to direct that big picture. Granted, everyone has had a day where, for whatever reason, we don't feel so good about ourselves and it seems that nothing will go right in any class. This temporary not-so-great feeling does impact the big picture, but only momentarily. What I'm talking about is the overall experience for the school year and a teaching career.

So many elements of our job are wrapped up in how we view ourselves and the job of educating students. How we view our own abilities, how we envision our own personal goals (plus those of our classrooms and schools) how we ask for advice or our inability to seek advice, how we receive criticism, what kind of team player we are, how much thought we give our job and our students and our lessons and plan, how much time we devote to planning those lessons, and how realistic we are about just what can be accomplished – all of these factors play into how well we as teachers direct that big picture.

So how do you view your own abilities? Well, if you are a licensed teacher, then you have dutifully completed not just many courses in your content area of expertise, but also numerous courses on how to impart knowledge, manage a classroom, address the different ways students learn, assess and document progress, score different types of assignments, word questions to assess understanding at different levels, etc. Depending on your level of experience at this point, you can probably write the perfect lesson plan in the correct format in your sleep. So, you ARE qualified to do this job! The problem comes with believing that you CAN do the job when you are loaded down with too many preps, too many students, not much administrative support, not enough sleep, and personal worries that no one at school knows anything about.

It really takes a huge amount of self-confidence to be a great teacher, and you wouldn't have pursued the field if you didn't start out with the confidence in your ability to do the job. But when the everyday routine becomes almost overwhelming, we must be diligent in giving ourselves daily reminders that we can do the job. What I would recommend is this: schedule into your day a time to find strength. Spend time with friends, exercise, be outside, or do whatever renews your spirit. As a Christian,

I find tremendous strength through several things. The ability to talk to God in prayer about my students and my feelings of inadequacy brings tremendous comfort and answers I need. I also find strength in reading the Bible, as I find personal, timely advice there. I also challenge myself to read books by seasoned educators, and I often enjoy downtime with other educators who have the same struggles. Much confidence comes just from hearing other educators say they have experienced the same struggles.

    In other words: don't neglect your own needs! Take a mental health day off every now and then to regain the perspective that you need and want, and you will be a much better teacher for it when you do return to your students.

THE HEART OF TEACHING

Chapter 6

WORKING WITH ADMINISTRATORS AND OTHER TEACHERS

Don't expect your principal to pump up your self-confidence every day. After all, you were hired because you are a licensed professional in the field of education, and as nice as daily perks and rewards would be, in the end it really is up to you to figure out how to encourage yourself. That being said, I do think it is part of the job of a more experienced teacher to encourage the newer teachers – every day if needed – to help them get through the first quarter, the first semester, the first year, the first time teaching a certain course, and so on. Unless you have been given an assignment to teach a class that is far out of your expertise, you DO know your material and so are quite competent to impart knowledge in this area. You **are** educated, and you have much information to share! That first year of teaching any class brings with it so much study, thinking, planning, preparation, and worry that it's hard to come up for air. But thankfully, the second and subsequent years tend to bring you the confidence and time that allow you to breathe while also tweaking or totally redoing your original plans.

Realizing that "it takes a village," you should be quick to seek advice in teaching. No matter what you're struggling with, other teachers have probably dealt with the same issue before and may have also figured out a solution. Don't reinvent if you don't need to, but also realize that human dynamics will differ between any two people, so be flexible and discerning when applying someone else's wisdom.

There are many ways in which this kind of advising among colleagues can be encouraged. For instance, if regular meetings of grade-level teachers aren't part of the plan at your school, then perhaps consider asking the principal to arrange a meeting or invite others who teach the same students as you to meet in your room. I have always found these meetings to be incredibly helpful, and for many reasons. For one thing, teachers who interact with your students at different times of the day often provide powerful insights into the students and the same behaviors you are experiencing. Be careful not to let these sessions become a student-bashing forum, though, and instead, strive to keep the focus on learning from each other so that you can all do a better job of serving the students. I have seen tremendous help for students coming from these meetings as teachers identify a pattern and then involve guidance counselors, administrators, or parents as needed to provide comprehensive support for that student.

Going back to the thought of underlying problems:

oftentimes one teacher has had a deep conversation with a student that sheds light on that student's behavior. Then, once those kinds of concerns are shared, or at least you know that the student is experiencing a rough stretch, all teachers involved are then better equipped to help that student.

As hard as it can be to accomplish, it's also important to try to develop a thick skin for taking criticism. This development is crucial if we are to grow in our chosen profession. We teachers are in charge of so much that it is very hard to take instruction. And rightly so, sometimes: many times, we may be thinking *how can someone else who hasn't spent time in my classroom know what I need to do?* Regardless of this, you will be criticized at various points and by various people, from students and parents to other teachers and administrators, and if you are prepared to learn from the experience and move on from it, that can save you from constant discouragement. Also, when you show that you can handle critiques and still be a team player with the students' best interests at heart, I sincerely believe that the people around you will see much less to criticize.

However, this also brings up the perennial problem of judgements based on snapshot observations. It is so hard to take criticism gracefully when it is handed down to you by an administrator who is judging from seeing just one short segment of time in your classroom. I remember one particular observation by a principal (who had very limited experience in the classroom) during a time when I was teaching a class of 24 students in a room that really should have had no more than 18 students in it. His main comment was that I should have moved around the room as I taught instead of standing in the front of the room. Well...if he had looked at the floor of the room, then maybe he would have realized that between all the tables and chairs, feet and book bags, there was no floor left for me to walk around on! I had also asked several times for a computer/projector remote, but still hadn't received it yet, so I needed to stay near my desk in order to advance slides using my mouse.

In that moment, considering the fact that this man had never held a teaching position himself helped me not get overly upset by his critiques. In your own case, if the criticism doesn't affect your job standing, then maybe it's better just to accept it humbly and let it go. But if the criticism is unjustified and could negatively affect your career, then you can certainly ask for a meeting, plan and deliver a calm, direct response to that criticism, and respectfully ask for another evaluation. I have found that calm, honest questions usually yield a listening ear from the administrator as well as their willingness to reconsider their initial thoughts and judgments.

Still, there will be times for every teacher that we will need to be helped or corrected. We are not perfect, and we never will be. Let me say that again – we are not perfect, and we never will be. In any school, it is the administrator's job to oversee how the students are dealt with, so when there is an issue, it is the administrator's job to bring it to light and address it. All the same, the more we develop respect for our students, the quicker we will be aware when we have messed up and the quicker we will be able to make things right so that an administrator doesn't need to get involved. In my experience, it tends to be when the teacher's pride is so great that they can't admit they could have handled things differently, that problems develop. So instead, be humble, be aware of what you say and how you say it, and if things do come out wrong, then be quick to acknowledge that, apologize, and move on.

As hard as it is to take criticism, though, it can be equally hard to give well-meaning criticism humbly. For instance, if I sense that another person really knows what they are talking about and has a kind word of exhortation for me, then I can take that advice anytime. The hardest requests or instructions for me to take are from administrators who have very little experience in the classroom yet are quick to tell me what to do or add yet another duty onto my long list. I think teachers in the public schools actually have better mechanisms in place for guarding against these sorts of demands, but at private schools, especially church-related ones, there is an added challenge in dealing with these demands as teachers are often viewed as doing ministry on top of a job, so they are not always treated with the same professional respect they are due. I don't think that the administrators of Christian schools set out to have this attitude, but because they often are so overworked themselves, they often need and expect their employees to provide services far beyond the official job description.

Whatever the case may be, I truly think that teachers should speak up when extra duties hamper their ability to do a good job in the classroom. If unrealistic expectations are never addressed, then how can an administrator be expected to deal with them? Likewise, it is my experience that administrators are usually glad to look for a solution if a teacher comes to them for help. Don't fume and complain while not actually asking for help. Not only does this make you frustrated and a less-effective teacher, but also it will totally take your focus off the students and put it onto poor you. This will hinder your job performance, and you still will not have even given administrators the chance to help you. Just like you cannot know what is troubling your students, it is also true that if you don't ask, your administrators can't know your thoughts unless you share them.

Teamwork is everything in education! I love being part of a team, and I love the camaraderie that comes with being a faculty member alongside other teachers who share the same goals and love the same kids. I truly think that having a team to be a part of is crucial to surviving as a teacher. My colleagues are often my best friends, and I count on them in so many ways to help me keep the right perspective on my job, my family, and more. I have cried with them over students and personal matters alike, and we have laughed so hard at ourselves that our students thought we were out of control! My colleagues continually encourage me to give my best as I hear about all the neat methods of learning that they are directing in their classes. Just having a fellow traveler who is sharing my exact journey is a wonderful source of encouragement!

As important as it is for us to have these relationships, both emotionally and professionally, I also think it is equally important for our students to see our interactions and to view us as normal, friendly people who have healthy relationships with each other as co-workers. Numerous times over the years, students have commented to me that they love seeing how much fun their teachers have together. They also love to hear anecdotes about their teachers and especially seem to notice close friendships.

For instance, I have the awesome and unique experience of teaching alongside a friend I have known since early childhood. The students already think it is neat that we are both named Dana, and it is always funny to watch their responses when we mention that we grew up together. For some students, I think it is the first time they realize that we were kids too, once upon a time!

However, I would be remiss if I didn't mention one particular caution in this section: we also need to be extremely careful not to speak disrespectfully of other teachers, and to not entertain negative comments that students make about their teachers. When I hear what I think might be a legitimate complaint about a teacher from a student, I usually suggest that the student go to the teacher respectfully and try to clarify their understanding. This generally results in a good ending with a calmer student (and oftentimes, calmer parents too). Also, when I hear something said in anger, I try to address that comment with the student in private after class and let them see how harmful a comment like that is. When you ask them how they would feel if they heard that a teacher had made a comment like that about them, they usually understand your point of showing them how hurtful it is to talk about others behind their backs.

THE HEART OF TEACHING

Chapter 7

HOW MY TEACHING CAN MAKE A DIFFERENCE

How seriously we take our job is directly reflected in how thoroughly we plan for our classes. Of course, the precise amount of planning required depends on so many things including the subject, whether labs are required, the students' ages, the class level, the class length (both in terms of the daily periods and the number of sessions overall), whether we have taught the lesson before, and so on. I think we can all agree that, when we began a career in education, we had NO IDEA how much planning and preparation is needed to get through just one day of school! And if anyone thinks they can get all their work done at school and take nothing home, I'm sorry to burst your bubble, but – it just doesn't work that way! When you respect your students and want to give them your best, though, it becomes much easier to spend the time needed to make your classes amazing for them.

A huge help for using preparation time efficiently is that most textbooks today come with incredible teacher books that have wonderful lesson planning ideas or even entire lessons planned out. If these lessons meet the goals for your classroom, use them! Don't reinvent if you don't have to, or if you don't have the time and energy! Plus, if you haven't been given a teacher help book to accompany the text, then ask for one to be ordered.

While I'm on that subject, too, make sure you take advantage of any test banks that are available. Especially for AP classes, these are truly time savers *and* life savers. (Or so it will feel, when you can scratch just one thing off your ever-present to-do list!) Don't feel you aren't doing your job professionally if you use these teaching aids. They will probably need some tweaking from you to personalize them for your classes, but they are definitely worth using and can help you tremendously, both in surviving a first year of teaching and then in using your time more efficiently in the years to come.

On a personal note, it seems to me that being a science teacher brings with it a need for even more preparatory work because of the need for laboratory exercises to reinforce the content and teach laboratory/research skills. And in overcrowded or space-locked schools, this is compounded by the fact that both labs and classrooms are full of students every period, and it is very difficult for a teacher to get uninterrupted time to set up a lab. Because of this problem at my school, for many years I have saved all my grading to take home with me and instead done only planning and preparation at school, in order to take advantage of being where the items I needed to teach my classes were. Oftentimes, this seemed the way to make the best use of my time at school. Having said that, it is always a struggle when I get home to prepare dinner and spend time with my family – and then need to get right back to work when my body and mind are begging me to relax (or to go to bed!). I totally understand why some science teachers (and teachers of any other subject, for that matter) almost give up on trying to provide hands-on activities for every unit – it just takes so much extra time for preparation! But the extra time taken is worth it for providing experiences that help young brains make connections and oftentimes, memories as well. Another nice thing about gaining experience, too, is that when you have taught a subject before you will need less prep time on the material and thus will have some extra time to plan the hands-on activities portion.

Regarding that idea of improving your lessons every year, it's also worth taking the time up front to make meticulous notes about what works and what you think you could do to improve the lesson, as you teach it. When we are in survival mode, we tend to auto-pilot from one day to the next and think only of the present. And that's understandable! But you will be so much better off the next time around if you take even just a few minutes each day to reflect and make notes for the next year or the next time you teach a particular class.

The students' ages and the level of the class – whether that's standard, honors, or AP – often dictate which methods of lesson presentation that its teachers should use. With the intense check-listing that teachers are encouraged to do to make sure their lessons and time with students include all the correct elements and the latest methods, we often feel that lecturing is not proper or efficient. But with higher-level classes and older students, interesting lectures are absolutely an accepted way of imparting knowledge. Even in lower-level classes and with younger students, sometimes a lecture is the most efficient way to present information, such as important groundwork information that must be stated clearly and understood fully before more complex concepts can build off it. But even the most mundane information can be made interesting if you are excited and relate the information to something personal and practical. Implementing an activity that involves everyone and helps them use the facts presented is a great way to follow a lecture and make sure the students remember the information.

There is no denying that technology has brought the greatest activities you can imagine to the classroom – but it has also brought about some of the most formidable challenges a teacher will face as well! Not only is a teacher expected to have a total grasp of the content, an understanding of the most effective ways to present the content and planned hands-on activities to enhance understanding, but also we are now expected to know and use resources and activities available online to further enhance understanding. This can add hours to planning for a lesson! In the best of scenarios, all the aspects of technology work and doing the online activity is a success. But if there are Wi-Fi issues, or problems with equipment, or computer screen fatigue on the part of our students, the activity becomes simply one more thing the students have to complete and isn't at all the enlightening experience we had hoped for. Aside from the occasional frustrations of technology, one very popular and rewarding use of technology in our school is using Google Classroom, which serves as a means of communicating with our students and allowing online submissions for assignments. Students get an immediate notification when a teacher posts a message on Google Classroom, which allows a teacher to remind students to bring textbooks that day, to meet in an alternate location, or to give them a heads-up about something exciting to be done in class.

When our administrators told us they wanted us to use computers in the classroom every day, if possible, I'll admit I was very frustrated at first since I had already given much time and thought to what I felt was a really great way of teaching my classes – without computers. In fact, I had a hard time getting past my own memories of the times when I had allowed computer usage that students would then use to pull up inappropriate sites, play games, or watch movies. But then I started making PowerPoint presentations (and then Google Slides when we moved solely to Google) from many lectures and tried as much as I could to bring computer use into the classroom – and I found that, especially for science, the lab simulations and demonstrations available online are incredibly helpful and fun. My younger colleagues were also extremely helpful in introducing me to many of the great websites that aid teaching and learning. There are so many time-saving practices already prepared and ready to go, so knowing about these can give you the resources to share when students need extra help. In addition, through trial and error our school has learned what sites need to be blocked and we are all very diligent in making sure that school computers aren't used for the wrong purposes.

An interesting and relevant anecdote here is a commentary on the overuse of PowerPoint presentations.

My own children were studying at universities at the same time that I was struggling with just how much to use computers and technology in my classes. So, I asked them about technology use in their college classrooms, and they told me about how it is integrated – but then all three also agreed that the best classes they remember most are the lectures or talks given by professors who are passionate about what they are teaching and just talk to their classes! I found that observation so interesting and have thought about it so many times as I got ready to teach a lesson. Technology can be a wonderful tool, but it is no substitute for a teacher who loves their subject and can't wait to tell their students about it! When a teacher is genuinely passionate about a subject and really enjoys talking about it, their students tend to respond positively and for the most part, behavior problems just don't surface. We can all think back to getting caught up in a speaker's excitement because their topic was of intense importance to them, and your students will do the same.

    Besides showing excitement for the subject, though, how else can we grab our students' attention? Well, for one thing, make the subject relevant! In other words, show your students why this information is important and how they can use it in real life. Every subject has a practical application, and by bringing this to your students' attention, you can answer the number one question posed by students everywhere: *Why do I need to know this?* Showing students the practicality of a subject and the potential uses of that information in everyday situations is a tremendous way of showing that you respect the fact that they will one day be adults. Honestly, I think that one of my favorite components of teaching is this very idea of showing students why the information I teach is needed for real life and in what careers they might use it. And yes, probably one of the best rewards I can earn is when a student chooses a major and career in one of the subjects that I have taught them!

Both within and beyond the classroom, opportunities abound for showing our students that we value them as human beings. In the hallway during class changes? Greet your students with eye contact and a warm *hello*! Honest compliments from teachers carry so much weight and can be just what a student needs to get through the day. Take joy in knowing your students and let them see that joy. They will read your face and your body language meticulously, so let your countenance display your inner love and respect for them.

THE HEART OF TEACHING

Chapter 8

SPECIFICALLY IN THE CLASSROOM

Okay, so thus far I've suggested that teachers who show respect to their students are much more successful in every way. And we've also established that we as teachers must respect ourselves and realize how much good we are bringing to the classroom. So how do these things actually take shape in the classroom? Or in other words: as a teacher, how should I think, act, and speak in the classroom in order to let the students know how much I respect and love them?

Well, first of all we must realize that we are capable of many things. On the one hand, we are capable of saying just the right thing to set a student on an exciting path for life – and on the other, we are just as capable of being sarcastic and totally taking the joy from a student who thought she finally got something right. We are also capable of neglecting a student who is hurting because we don't want to take time to care, or we don't want to get behind in our plans. However, we are given tremendous power when we become teachers, and it can take all the maturity and self-control we have developed – and then some! – to use that power for good. What opportunities we are given just by the fact that we are with these students every day! We have the chance to see their strengths developing and we can encourage them by pointing out these strengths and suggesting how they might use them within the school setting, and maybe beyond it in a career as well. I will never forget telling a young man as a 9th grader that he had leadership qualities and I would love to see him in student leadership at our school. These words prompted him to run for student council for both the 10th and 11th grades, and then for the coveted position of being a member of the Executive Leadership Council as a senior. He was elected each year and developed great public relations skills as well as confidence in persuasive and public speaking. At the end of his senior year, his father came to me to thank me for encouraging his son. Just simple words, maybe, but what meaningful encouragement all the same! There is nothing like the high that comes when you run into a student years after you have taught them and hear that student tell you that something you said affected them deeply and changed their whole trajectory in life. There is also no low like the one where you said something you greatly regret, and you didn't get a chance to set things straight. So don't have regrets! Don't ever tear down, and instead look for opportunities to build up! Apologize if what you say causes hurt or discouragement. Always be ready to make things right.

    In any leadership position, power and authority

can only operate positively when combined with humility and the ability to recognize when you are in the wrong. We may say the wrong things – though hopefully, less and less as we grow as teachers – but because of our failings, we must be willing to say "I'm sorry" whenever necessary, even if that means many times a day. Our students need to see that we are human and make mistakes, but more importantly, they need to see the value of humility and how we take responsibility for the wrongs we say and do. Just like in parenting, we will NOT always be right, so we need to acknowledge when we fail so that our students can learn from us in these situations. Acting as if we are always right is NOT a good character trait, but being honest and owning the consequences when we fail IS. It also helps to be able to laugh at yourself. For example, if you've made a simple mistake like leaving out the correct answer for a multiple-choice question on a test, then turn it into a positive by putting the right answer on the board, giving them the points, and then commenting on how it was only your 3rd mistake for the year, so you're doing pretty well overall. Students love to laugh WITH you, so take every opportunity to give them that chance. How wonderful if every student could see this modeled in school before they assume positions in society, particularly leadership roles! Imagine leaders and bosses who are quick to take responsibility for their actions and admit when they are wrong. Just this one ability would change so many workplaces for the better, and with them, both society and the world as well. Also, dealing with mistakes humorously can bring everyone a smile and that very action of smiling makes each person feel better, so not only have you shown a powerful lesson in humility, but also you have brightened the classroom atmosphere.

If we are humble then we also can be teachable, which is another important trait of a great teacher. I should be ready to learn something new from my students – and to acknowledge it when I do. Can you imagine the incredible boost a student gets when you say, "That is amazing! I didn't know that! Where did you learn that?" When we get excited over a presentation that is well done, we just might be providing the encouragement that a budding scientist or historian needs to realize that they are smart and able to contribute to the knowledge imparted in their class. Plus, not only is their confidence boosted, but also they feel like an integral part of the class. This is an important trait to develop in order to function and learn adeptly in a college classroom and then later, to contribute to the workplace as well.

Students also need to see the enlightenment that you experience when, as an adult, you are learning something new. I think that sometimes we give a false impression that there is a set amount of learning to be done in each subject and that because we have been to college, we know everything that we need to. How much more beneficial both for students and for society at large to foster the recognition that we need to keep learning throughout our entire lives! On a related note, don't feel that you need to be an expert on every project topic, and don't be afraid to let a student follow a rabbit trail if they are very interested in a subject. I have had students end up studying a topic in graduate school that they first researched in my biology or psychology classes. We never know how our encouragement will affect our students' interests and studies.

New knowledge is great, and we can always learn more, but just as important as being teachable in content is being teachable in terms of how students learn, what you can do to facilitate that learning even more, what confuses them, and what might make the lesson more interesting. I truly value what my students think, and I want them to have some ownership in our class. In my classes, it is a common occurrence for me to ask after a unit, lab, or even a daily activity, "how could this be improved?" or "what would make this better?" Some of my best teaching activities have come from mulling over comments made by my students and incorporating their ideas into what I need to cover next time. We should never be afraid to ask our students' opinions. We are still in charge of all aspects of the learning experience, and our experience and professional know-how should guide us into knowing what is practical. But there is no harm in giving the students more buy-in by applying their suggestions when possible. We all know how much better we enjoy a situation and how much easier it is to invest when we feel our thoughts are heard and respected.

With each presentation of new knowledge, make it a priority to present that information in several different ways so that, hopefully, you are helping all types of learners better assimilate the material. Say the terms in the lecture, write key words on the board, have the students write about that key material on their papers, and demonstrate the concept if possible. Examples of concepts are wonderful ways to build our memories, but at the same time, good ones take time to think up, so when possible, allow enough planning time to develop and provide great examples. Remember, too, that there is no harm in saying

"I can't think of a good example right now, but I will have one for you tomorrow" – and then make sure that you *do* follow through and are ready the next day. Throughout the year, I also try to invite my students to share with me what they think would help them learn better. Some students do well with guided notes, while others like to write their own. Some like Google Slides, and some prefer for a teacher to just talk to them. Some students learn better from their peers' explanations, so group work suits them best. For me, the key is variety, so that everyone gets to experience their easiest way of learning. The students know this is why I rarely have two classes in a row that are the same format, but even those who need more structure adjust quickly, as they know I am trying to accommodate the needs of every student.

 Something that demonstrates respect to students more than just about anything else is when we are secure enough in our long-term planning to be flexible with our lesson presentation or to change up lessons entirely if the students give you a workable request. Some of the best lessons I think I have ever taught were when the weather was beautiful, and instead of sitting in the classroom we went outside to talk as we walked. Some teachers' plans and content just won't work with going outside like this, but I think we all can insert a little something fun to brighten up our audiences. If you have trouble deviating from your plans, then ask yourself whether, in the grand scheme of things, a change-up really matters. If the kids know you will adjust your plan when you can in order to accommodate a valid request, then they will also respect you when you say that you can't.

 One way I often deviate from my set lesson plan is by

addressing current events and contemporary issues. This can be done in many different ways. Simply mentioning and acknowledging an event can at least help the students realize there is life outside of their own. I usually go deeper by bringing up a news article on a disaster or other event currently taking place in the world and using that teachable moment to dig deeper into volcanoes, hurricanes, tornadoes, or whatever is happening. This is easily done in science classes, but just about any current event can be discussed within a particular discipline. Within any subject area you teach, let your students brainstorm on the implications of that current even or give them 5 minutes on their computers to research some implications within your discipline and then discuss what they find.

One reason why I love teaching Environmental Science is because it is so easy to integrate current events and political discussions into our class sessions. Some of my favorite classes are those where I give out topics that are currently being discussed or dealt with all around the world. The students have 15 minutes to research the answers to some questions I provide, then we make a circle with our chairs or go sit in a sunny nook in the hallway and each student tells the class what they have learned. It is always interesting to me how, after researching, the students realize that a good amount of information should be looked at and much more time spent researching before they start to form an opinion. This realization alone has led to some interesting discussions and challenges as the students started to think more critically about situations rather than basing their opinions just on what they had heard. I try to never discredit parents' beliefs when these are brought up, but I do want the students to understand that there are intelligent, well-meaning people who might totally disagree with an established scientific opinion because they haven't fully studied it, so the students owe it to themselves, and ultimately society, to make sure that they have a strong understanding of all aspects of an issue before they establish a strong opinion about it.

As we've already seen, there are so many ways in which we can show respect to our students. Think about all your interactions in the classroom alone, from your first greeting of the day to the end of class. These are all opportunities! Speak to your students when they enter the room. Greet them by name and ask something personal, even simply "how is your day going"? Some of the most engaging teachers I have ever observed started their classes with a challenge on the board. This makes settling in for the class more efficient and starts the engagement of students' minds even before the bell rings. I love to have a brain teaser on the board or on their desks at the start of class to help that all-important critical thinking develop. I might do this only once a week to keep it special, but after a bit, the kids will ask for one almost every day.

Whatever the method, I think it is so important to engage with the students in some personal way at the start of class. A dear friend and colleague is well-known for her "Thorns and Roses" exercise, in which each student mentions one thorn, or frustrating thing going on in their life, and then one rose, which is a good thing going on in their life. My friend uses this only occasionally, but what a great way to let the students know you care and that they matter! Also, the insights you can gain through hearing about their struggles and their successes is incredibly helpful, as you seek to teach them on many levels.

Sound teaching practices enter the picture here by starting class with a good review of previous material and questioning to pique their interest. Trying to make sure students have a good understanding of material previously taught shows tremendous respect for students. This is hard, especially if you have students of differing abilities in your class, but you should still try to do the best you can. It's always difficult to know when to keep moving ahead and when to regroup and redo, and this simple exercise can help. Also, talking over effective reviewing techniques with a more experienced teacher in your department will never be time wasted, and your ability to keep moving all students ahead will develop quickly the more you teach.

As stated before, vary your lesson presentations as much as you can, so that all different learning styles can be accommodated, and students will have chances to learn in the ways that they find most useful. Visual examples can be the hardest examples to find, but the reward is well worth the research you'll have to do, since most kids remember best if they both see and hear information. Guided notes and other organizational helps are also great tools for helping kids stay focused. Every now and then, try to have a day where the students are given research topics and allowed to work on their own or in groups. After hearing my own children mention to me several times how much group work they had to do in college and graduate school and how high school kids need to learn to work in groups, I have tried to incorporate group work with every level of class I taught. This takes constant involvement from you as the teacher to ensure that all members of the group are engaged, but with some practice, most kids rise to the challenge and come to enjoy contributing. This type of activity works incredibly well with my AP Environmental students, who have produced some amazing group projects on case studies. I am so proud of these students, since I change the makeup of the groups with every project and they all work equally as hard no matter who is in the group. It feels good thinking that these kids will be the leaders and presenters of their groups in college, and subsequently in their jobs and society.

All things considered, the amount of time and thought I put into planning assessments of my students' understanding of the material says much about how much I respect them. If I hardly put any time into writing questions and don't prepare short answer and essay questions thoughtfully, then I can count on frustrated students who feel I have not fairly tested them on the material we covered in class. As in teaching, on assessments try to vary the types of questions used and have questions at all levels of thinking, from simple recall to critical analysis. Every now and then throughout the year, I also try to insert humor into a test, and at least once a year I will use each student's name on a test. I try to do this as well on semester and final exams, just to break the tension and hopefully help the students relax. It makes my day when I hear the kids start giggling at their desks! To me, that is well worth the extra time needed to make sure I don't leave anyone out.

Another way of showing respect is how well you listen to students. Ideally, when a student approaches us as teachers with something they want to talk about, we have no other pressing needs so we can put everything down and listen. But during a normal school day when you are responsible for so many students, it can be really challenging to give one your undivided attention. However, I've found that if I don't have the time or energy to really listen to a student, it's better to tell them so and then to schedule a different time to talk or suggest they go to someone else who can help them immediately. This simple honest answer can teach the student a number of things, including assessing the importance of what they want to share and considering whether it is urgent enough to interrupt a teacher's day. It also shows respect by telling the student you really cannot help them right then, but also that you care enough to tell them who can or by setting aside time later just for them.

    I also love to have review sessions in my classes where every student gets called on. They can have their notes and their books open in front of them and I am careful to ask each student a question that is at their level of understanding. I've also found that one of the best ways to engage every student is to call them either Dr. or Professor, using the title and their last name when you ask them a question. Even the seniors love this, and it seems to put them in a good mood and help them concentrate. While we are talking about reviewing material, another good way to engage the students is to have each one ask YOU a question from their notes. Give them time to look through their notes before you do this, and hopefully they will ask you about something they don't understand.

    Going back to technology for a minute – I've also found that playing a Kahoot game from Kahoot.com is a great way to review material at the end of a class. There are also numerous other online games and reviews available that are just as much fun while also being productive for reviewing material. For instance, I use a rousing Kahoot game as a reward for work well done and the students don't ever want to stop playing. It doesn't take much time to enter questions and answers from the topics we have just covered, and sometimes I am lucky enough to find a ready-made quiz or game that is exactly what I need. Another fun thing to do is this - when you get ready to play, have each student choose a screen name that goes with the subject you're reviewing. For example, when we study the properties of waves, students can choose a name like wavelength, trough, crest, etc.

  Yet another way in which I show my students that I respect them is by having them design labs or demonstrations that they can share with younger students. We then invite a class over from the Lower School and my students set up stations where they teach small groups of students who rotate from station to station. I don't know who enjoys this more, my students or the younger ones. The older students are so proud of what they have done, and I love that they have learned a concept or principle well enough to be comfortable demonstrating it.

  Even the negatives can teach us all something, though. In fact, when you have taught a lesson that you felt was a flop, I think it does wonders for your credibility to be honest with your students the next day and say that the lesson did not go at all like you wanted it to. Go over the material again to make sure the students understand it and then ask them for suggestions on doing the lesson the next year. I think when we are honest about our frustrations that affect the classroom, students develop a greater respect for us and a greater appreciation for the work we do to teach them. Our students need to see humility modeled. Some adults don't seem able to say "I made a mistake" or "I'm sorry," and how good it is for our students to see someone in authority taking responsibility or admitting that they feel they could do better!

THE HEART OF TEACHING

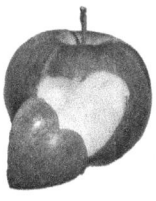

Chapter 9

MORE TANGIBLE THINGS I CAN DO

As we have seen, the measure of respect that we have for our students can be seen in intangible things like the way we greet and welcome them, the words we speak to them, and the lessons we have planned. The food for thought that we post in our classrooms and the topics that we ask them to think about can also show them that we know and expect they can think deeply about things. But sharing some of what is important to us can also show that we trust them enough to bring them into our world.

Sharing limited, appropriate personal stories with them and using yourself as an example can help your students feel a kinship with you. Let the students know you were not a perfect kid or student, that you definitely made (and continue to make!) mistakes, and that you understand that nobody is perfect. When they see that you accept and respect yourself even when you have goofed in many ways, it will help them toward accepting and respecting who they are as well, often in tremendously positive ways. For instance, when they understand that becoming the person you want to be not only takes great effort and work, but also that it is a worthy goal for even an esteemed teacher, then they will incorporate that goal into their long-range plans without you having to preach to them about it.

    Classroom atmosphere is so important for showing students that we care, and also for making them feel accepted and cared about so that they can learn. It seems to me that elementary teachers have this area totally mastered, but I think upper-school teachers often need some help in this area. I do understand that the older the students get, the less they need the decorations and attention-getters on the walls, but the overall atmosphere can still have a huge impact on both their state of mind and their ability to concentrate. I have always tried to have beautiful artwork in my classroom like Monet prints or unique pictures I have collected in the course of my travels, and I have always decorated my walls with pictures of our incredible natural landmarks, like the Grand Teton mountains, Yosemite, Monument Valley, etc., which often prompt great conversations before and after class. For the last five years, I have been lucky to be in classrooms that lent themselves more to "ambiance design" than the large open biology lab where I used to teach, so I have really enjoyed setting up comfortable, cozy classrooms. One year I painted walls in accent colors, hung

More Tangible Things I Can Do

a large colorful tapestry to cover another wall, and hung a second, beautifully-woven butterfly tapestry from one of our Costa Rica senior trips over a bulletin board. With help from IKEA, I color-coordinated everything I could on and around my desk, scattered 4 lamps around the room and one on my desk, and – probably the most important – every day I had some kind of fragrance emitter working that made the room smell SO good. Later on, the students could also give input on what scents we should have, and for many of them, their first choice was some kind of vanilla or cinnamon fragrance, which they said made them think of homemade cookies! On a daily basis different kids, including students I didn't even teach, would come into the room to close their eyes and just breathe. They would say they just needed to relax. And I heard so many times, "Mrs. K., I just love coming into your room! It makes me feel so good!" So yes, I spent some money to do it, but it has been worth every penny!

I also take advantage of every holiday I can to decorate. What actually put the thought in my mind to do this was discovering the 70% and 80% off clearance items after a holiday. After seeing garlands of fall leaves going for just a few dollars, I realized that I could do a lot of decorating that could be reused year after year for not much money at all. Now, yes, I do this for the students, but I think just as importantly, I also do it for me. It just makes me smile every morning when I turn on the lights and see my classroom as a sort of cozy retreat. What a great way to get ready for the students to come! And again, yes, I spend money on this ambiance, but when I found I could get a strand of 100 small lights from Michael's for $2.50, I was sold on decorating for every special day!

Fall is easy to celebrate with orange lights and fall flowers and leaves. Those decorations could also work for Thanksgiving with the addition of a few pumpkins and other things, and then of course, Christmas is easy! I put lights all over the room – around the white boards, hanging from the ceiling, around bulletin boards and windows, and everywhere I can get them in. And yes, I even have a Christmas tree, though it is small - a 4-foot tall one. One year after Christmas, I went to a dollar store and was so excited to find ornaments, garlands, and lights in our school colors – royal blue and white – at 90% off! So, from then on, the Christmas tree also became a year-round school spirit tree decked out all in blue and white. Winter with snowflakes and white lights, Valentine's Day, and spring were all times to be celebrated with lights and flowers as well. So many little efforts, but they each have a great impact!

You don't have to do all the decorating I do in order to have a successful classroom, but it is just a natural thing for me to do, as I love having color and beauty around me. I also feel that I have been repaid many times for my money spent and the time I spend in decorating by the kids telling me how much they loved that I do decorate and how it lifts their spirits. So, if my decorating does anything to help them feel more positively about their educational experience and help make great memories for them, then any trouble I go to is well worth it.

An amazing discovery I just happened upon was the value of having large stuffed animals in my classroom – yes, even at the upper grade levels! This came about because I had taken a group of students to the South Carolina Zoo one weekend, and they bought me a large stuffed tiger at the museum shop. I named her India and perched her on top of my file cabinet in the classroom. Well, it wasn't long until the kids were having friendly arguments over who got to hold her during class. I never saw this coming and found it really interesting because generally the kids who had trouble concentrating were the ones who wanted to hold her, and they literally snuggled her the entire class without making a sound. So, after that I got up in our attic and took out some of my kids' large stuffed animals and – after getting their permission, of course – took them to school to be added to our classroom zoo. What a hit! Now instead of one tiger being fought over, there were probably seven animals all around the room, usually in someone's arms. I was absolutely amazed that high school students didn't care who saw them sitting in class with a stuffed animal in their arms! The whole idea may sound silly to you, but I am a witness to the fact that restless students can focus when they are holding onto a large stuffed animal. I have picked up some great animals at thrift shops too, though I do put them in the freezer for several days to kill off any microscopic stowaways before I introduce them to my classroom.

  At my current high school, we have block classes several days a week. This extra time has allowed for some fun lunch times for the classes that meet right before or after the lunch break. Occasionally we will take up money and order pizza to be delivered to us and eat in our classroom. I keep a stash of paper plates, napkins, and cups in my room and will bring in inexpensive store-brand sodas to drink. What a treat for the kids – they really look forward to it, and it is so easy to do! Every few weeks, I also make muffins or a coffee cake for my morning classes.

I found out quickly that if you feed the teenagers in your classes, they will do anything you ask of them for the rest of class. Plus, what a great way to tell them how much you like them! I also remember the teacher of an AP workshop once saying she would buy day-old big cookies or other desserts on sale when she saw them and put them in her freezer. Then when she felt everyone needed a pick-me-up, she would get out a dessert and it would be thawed by the time she wanted to surprise her students. I love treating my students with food because I think of how much my children would have enjoyed their teachers treating them and how much I would have enjoyed this as a student.

Well, I may have said this before, but the bottom line in being a successful teacher is having the perspective that this job is not about us. It is all about educating and showing love and respect to the children we are blessed to walk alongside, so that they can then make a difference in someone else's life as well as their own.

Because my school is a small private school, every year we have opportunities to take class trips. This gives students and teachers the chance to work together in a different setting without the normal classroom restraints, which means getting to laugh and work together on mutual projects and equal ground. I have treasured these times greatly, as my friendships with both teachers and students have grown while we have worked together and had fun together. On this note, if it is possible at your school, field trips in your subject area are awesome chances to have great conversations with students away from school. They are a lot of work to plan, but the benefits reach far beyond the academic value. In fact, graduates who return for a visit when they are home from college talk more about the memories of off-campus activities than they do the classroom!

But what can you substitute for field trips when it is difficult to schedule them? Turn a day or two every quarter into a field trip day – even if that's just inside your classroom or school. Invite an energizing speaker or another class, show a movie complete with popcorn and drinks, have a scavenger hunt, decorate with a theme, order pizza to be delivered...the possibilities are endless. To help yourself remember to do these fun days, make yourself a small sign for your desk that says "Make Great Memories!" Yes, these events take extra planning, but by the time you are ready to implement them, you will be as excited about that special activity as the kids are.

One of my favorite activities to do with my biology students is to take two days to learn from a YouTube video that walks viewers through the steps of drawing a lion's head. In this way, I can introduce scientific illustration as a career, reinforce the need to look and listen for details, and teach some principles of drawing all at the same time. But by far the best part of this activity is that students who are convinced they are not the least bit artistic end up with a beautiful pencil drawing of a lion - and they are so excited with their drawings! I then encourage the kids to display their artwork somewhere or give them to another teacher, and it just makes my day when I see one of the drawings on another teacher's wall or hanging in pride of place inside a locker.

THE HEART OF TEACHING

Chapter 10

THE PARENT TEACHER PARTNERSHIP

My oldest child just turned 32 this summer. I am sure I could have been a better parent in a lot of areas, but regardless, I certainly learned a few things about being a parent from my kids and their situations that are worth passing on. Couple this with what I've learned from years of experience in dealing with parents as an educator, and I feel well qualified to express my opinions on how parents and teachers can partner with one another to create a great school experience for students.

Believe me, I have made my share of mistakes – both as a parent and as a teacher. I am ashamed to admit that more than once, when I've gotten angry emails from parents, I've had to think that I am just getting my payback, as I've sent my own fair share of those too. It is so easy, and only natural, to react as a parent when you feel that your child has been treated unfairly. But it isn't fair to the teacher – or indeed, right as a parent – to react hastily and with malice, even in these situations.

    As a teacher, I have had experiences with parents who ranged all along the spectrum of involvement with their kids' education. While at a public school, I did have parents who cared very much about the learning experiences and education their children were receiving, but I also had several parents who told me never to send assignments home, especially books, because they didn't want their child to waste time on schoolwork there. This was so sad to me because, of course, those children had such potential that could have become reality with a little encouragement from their parents.

    I have also dealt with a few parents, especially in private school settings, who seemed to start the school year with a mentality of us vs. them. From day one, I have been questioned about why I do things, why I said what I did, and why I looked at a child when I said a certain thing. I've also been reminded, more than once, that the parent is paying my salary, with the implication that this salary could be withheld if I didn't comply with certain demands. As a teacher I have also been yelled at, sent nasty and threatening emails, and even had one parent demand my resignation for writing honest answers on a medical form that I had been asked to complete. Each of these affronts happened because the parent in question did not take the time to find out why I said or did what I had – or sometimes, even *IF* I had actually said or done what they were accusing me of.

    The good news is that, in many more situations than these few exceptions, I have had the honor and privilege of working with parents to instill values in their children that will help these young people develop into outstanding adults. Honestly, this kind of partnership is another of the highlights of my teaching experience. Being able to share the joy of success and growth in a young person is so inspiring and extremely satisfying! And from a parental standpoint, there is not much that brings me as much peace and appreciation as realizing that another adult sees the same potential that I do in my child and is also encouraging and helping my child in ways that I can't. This is the same reason why I love running into the parents of students I have taught in the past and hearing how well they are now doing in college, graduate school, or the workplace. Many of these parents have become lifelong friends as we have shared an important common goal. And these encounters just confirm that I am doing both what I want to do and also what I feel God's purpose in life for me is – to make a difference so that someone else's life will be productive and rewarding.

What I would stress in this area, then, is that good teachers want nothing more than to partner with parents in the ongoing education of their children. Likewise, good schools should encourage this partnership from the start of school every year. In my own experience, nearly every teacher I know counts it a privilege to work with students and parents and they are available whenever they are not teaching to answer questions and offer help and advice to parents and students. Teachers want to be on good terms with parents, and there are many ways of helping make that kind of relationship happen.

As amazing as this relationship can be, though, I know that there are also obstacles that can stand in its way. For instance, on my own part I know that I've made the mistake of listening only to my upset child and then sounding off in an email to a teacher before finding out the other side of the situation. In this case, how much more mature it would be to acknowledge to the teacher that your child is upset and then ask if they can shed any light on the situation to help you know how to better guide your child. More often than not, there has been a misunderstanding on the part of one or both parties involved, and your simple request for clarification can do much to begin addressing the problem.

    Truly, I think that the first step in teachers partnering with parents is making sure from the beginning of class that parents know you welcome their correspondence and insights in dealing with their children. Sending a letter home at the beginning of the school year, greeting parents and students warmly at open houses, sending a general note home after the first week of class saying how much you are enjoying getting to know their children – all of these things can go a long way toward making a parent feel like they are an integral part of their child's experience in school. If you have time too, a personal note sent to parents early in the school year telling them something positive about their child is a huge confidence-builder for parents and student alike. In this situation, if the student knows that you see good in them and you are not out to get them in trouble, generally the result is a very teachable young person as well as a positive relationship between teacher and student.

    I do have colleagues who send weekly letters home with their students, discussing what has been done in their class. For them, that is great! For me, though, I know that I never seem to find the time or the energy on Friday to put together this kind of letter. Plus, I've also had parents comment that they receive so many emails from the school that they don't read them all – it's just too much to keep up with. So personally, I want to find a good balance, making sure that parents have a good sense of how their children are doing while also not overwhelming them with smaller communications. This way, I find, the really important must-have conversations don't get ignored by accident. Most recently, I've found that I prefer to communicate what I do in class by giving parents the link to my Google Classroom site at the beginning of the year. This is where I post my syllabi that include reading assignments, project assignments, and due dates. Then when they have questions about particulars such as due dates, I can refer them to that site so that they can peruse it on their own time and in as much detail as they need.

There are exceptions to this, of course. Every now and then when we do a unique activity, I take some pictures and send them home with a note saying how much I am enjoying working with the kids. I got my inspiration for doing this from an AP Psychology teacher who worked with my daughter during her junior year. I don't think I had gotten any correspondence from any teachers before that point, so when an email from a teacher came in the middle of the morning, I was more than a little nervous, wondering if something was wrong. How wrong I was! It was just a lovely little note saying that the class was building neurons from candy that the teacher had provided, and how blessed the teacher felt that we had shared our kids with her, plus how well they were working together on this project and just how much she enjoyed working with them overall. It was so clear from her note that she not only loved and respected the students, but also that she appreciated us, the parents. I will never forget how good that note made me feel, how thankful I was that my daughter was in her class and how much my respect for her as a teacher grew!

There are many ways in which I now use these kinds of insights in my own work. For instance, whenever I do have an issue with a student, I've found that it is so helpful to immediately write the parents a quick note telling them what happened and asking for their insight into what may have caused the problem. Most of the time, the parents are so thankful that I wrote, and they can often shed some light on a difficult situation going on at home or perhaps in the student's life specifically. In this way, a simple act of communication can usually get everyone involved on the same page and help the teacher focus on the perspective of meeting students' needs.

Here it is also worth noting that the parents who are never satisfied unless their child is getting an A are often the ones who ride their children so hard and instill fear in them rather than respect. Most seasoned teachers will tell you that they can quickly spot the students whose parents are never satisfied, as these children tend to have very little confidence in their own abilities. It is worth noting as well that a higher socioeconomic background also does not imply better parenting. In fact, it often seems that the wealthier parents are the ones who give material things to their children rather than providing situations where those children can learn and grow. The full nuances of this topic are probably best left to sociologists to discuss at greater length, but the point can still be made that better parenting happens when parents have long-term goals for their children and plan on how to instill values in them, rather than simply reacting to the child's wants and giving them things instead of imparting lasting qualities.

THE HEART OF TEACHING

Chapter 11

DAILY REMINDERS TO HELP US KEEP THE PROPER PERSPECTIVE

Sometimes I find myself feeling pretty selfish, and I have a little mental pity party for myself and other teachers who invest such great amounts of time, money, and emotion – sometimes even sacrificing the extras we could be enjoying in our own lives – all so that we can stay in a lower-paying job. However, I also try not to let these feelings last too long because they're not fair to either my students or myself, and over the course of my teaching career, I've found that there are certain thoughts that I can dwell on instead to help me put things back in the proper perspective. I have even written some of these thoughts on index cards as reminders on my desk, and I share them here so my fellow teachers can use them too to encourage you to maintain a respectful perspective.

1 - Every student is precious and deserves my respect and

best efforts.

2 - Every student is valuable to the school and class, bringing a unique perspective that is just as valuable as anyone else's.

3 - I am not better than my students and I am not worth more than they are.

4 - I should take joy in knowing these young people and having a part in shaping their lives.

5 – I should remember how it feels to be a teenager. Encouragement from an adult can yield tremendous results!

6 – I should remember how good it feels to make a positive difference in these kids' lives. That feeling is worth all the work that it takes to make that difference.

7 - You may think you are doing all the teaching, but you should also open yourself up to learning from your students today.

8 - Your students' opinions matter! Listen to them and create an atmosphere that helps them understand an issue before they shape their opinions on it. Help them understand how important it is to fully understand an issue.

9 - Your students deserve to be heard as much as you do.

10 - No act of kindness goes unrewarded. Whatever energy you have to give, let it be used in loving and giving to your students!

11 - Reflect on this: what did we ever do to merit being born in a free country, where we have the privilege of going to school and learning what we need to become productive, respected and contributing members of society? Don't waste this opportunity, for yourself or for your students!

12 - Every student is unique, and it is my job to encourage the gifts that each student brings to the world. We have no idea of the potential each child has, so we should pour as much guidance, information, and encouragement as we can into each one so that we have done our jobs fully.

13 - Remember, you are not the reason for a student's existence, and each one has an entire life going on outside your classroom. Don't overload them with work as if your class is all that matters. They are not robots – they are multifaceted young people who need free time too so they can still be kids.

14 - These students are not our projects to rebuild. They are valuable in their own right! Instead, we should look for how we can positively contribute to their successes, being just one of the many people who will cross paths with them in their journeys.

15 - Realize that you won't be able to help or reach every student. Sometimes their circumstances or emotional state will keep your voice from being heard, but keep in

mind again that no act of kindness goes unrewarded. Your love and respect will make a difference in their lives, even if it is a small one.

16 - Don't sweat the small stuff. Allow your students to be kids. If you take offense at everything or expect them to be just like you, then you will never be satisfied and your students will feel like they can never please you.

17 - Choose your battles carefully. Don't be hard-nosed and headstrong in situations that don't really matter. Ask yourself "In the grand scheme of things, does this really matter?"

18 - After thinking through the actions of your day, if you feel that you made a mistake or over-reacted, then do what you need to do to make things right. Apologize if necessary, clarify what you said or meant, and make sure that you can live with whatever that decision was.

19 - Make the classroom experience fun for yourself as well as the students. If you are having fun, the students can't help but feel the excitement too.

20 - Life is short, so use every day you are given. When we teach, numerous opportunities are placed right before us to make a difference, encourage a child, and reinforce their worth as an individual. Enjoy the students you interact with. Celebrate their abilities and uniqueness. Just love them!

Chapter 12

CONCLUSION

I wrote the first 11 chapters of this book during the year before the COVID - 19 pandemic totally disrupted normal life and school. Then the pandemic hit and school as we had known it changed drastically as we switched to online teaching and learning. It was as if the rug was pulled out from under us and all my methods that were tied to the classroom atmosphere didn't apply anymore. Of course, even with online learning, the things we said and our demeanor could show respect, but especially with large classes, it was very difficult to interact with every student during an online session. We were all aware of the need to limit screen time so we didn't want to say more than was absolutely necessary in a session. I still tried to have a sense of humor and make the learning atmosphere more interesting by being in a different location every class, hiding a gnome in the background for the kids to find, and designing some of the most creative projects I had ever produced. But for me at least, these things were no substitute for the personal interactions I had enjoyed in the classroom. Because of my struggles, I have the highest admiration for the teachers who were able to be very effective educators in the online learning situation, and I am sure there are those much more competent than me in online education who have some great ideas for engaging and encouraging your students during an online class.

    Even when some of us were able to come back to the classroom, changes were required that greatly altered the atmosphere of the classroom. Out of necessity for our health and safety, we were all wearing masks, cleaning continually, socially distancing, unable to do much group work, and basically limited to just doing the most sterile and individual exercises of information dissemination. As much as we wanted to think we could still make a difference in lives, our jobs seemed to consist of delivering endless reminders to students to wear their masks correctly or even to put their masks on, and to move apart to keep from spreading the virus. Amidst all of this, how could we even think of anything beyond just surviving an unimaginably difficult situation? So, I parked this manuscript in my Google Docs for a while, as it just seemed to hold little relevance in the online and COVID classroom.

    But now that most of us are physically able to be with our students again, and now that we are better able to cope with and adjust to what is needed to keep us all healthy, I have pulled my thoughts out of storage with the hope that these ideas can provide encouragement for showing our students the respect they deserve, so that they learn all they can and grow up to become positive contributors

Conclusion

for the benefit of others. Consider what can happen if we model treating others with respect, and our students in turn see the value of those around them and develop an attitude of respect toward those they will serve as adults. What a valuable contribution we will make to a world that desperately needs to put aside differences and work together for the common good. And of course, there is no greater joy than seeing your students go out and make the world a better place!

THE HEART OF TEACHING

www.ingramcontent.com/pod-product-compliance
Lightning Source LLC
Chambersburg PA
CBHW071505070526
44578CB00001B/444